GREAT PETS

Big Dogs

Joyce Hart

Marshall Cavendish
Benchmark
New York

With thanks to Scott R. Miner, DVM, for his expert review of the manuscript.

Marshall Cavendish Benchmark
99 White Plains Road
Tarrytown, New York 10591-9001
www.marshallcavendish.us

Library of Congress Cataloging-in-Publication Data
Hart, Joyce, date
Big dogs / by Joyce Hart.
p. cm. — (Great pets)
Summary: "Describes the characteristics and behavior of big dogs as pets,
also discussing the physical appearance and place in the history of big
dogs"—Provided by publisher.
Includes bibliographical references and index.
ISBN 978-0-7614-2707-0
1. Dogs—Juvenile literature. I. Title.
SF426.5H373 2008
636.7—dc22
2007013042

Front cover: A yellow Labrador retriever
Title page: A dalmatian
Back cover: A Leonberger

Photo research by Candlepants, Inc.
Front Cover: Mark Raycroft/Minden Pictures
The photographs in this book are used by permission and through the courtesy of:
Photo Researchers Inc.: Susan Kuklin, 1, 24; Robert Noonan, 22; Jacana, 26.
©2007 Ei Katsumata at www.worldofstock.com: 6. *SuperStock:* Bridgeman Art Library, London, 4;
age fotostck, 7, 30; David Muscroft, 13; Jerry Shulman, 21. *Corbis:* Jim Craigmyle, 8; DLILLC, 12;
Olivier Maire/epa, 16; Paul A. Souders, 25; Nation Wong/zefa, 28; John Periam; Cordaiy Photo Library Ltd., 34;
Ariel Skelley, 37. *AP Images:* Chris O'Meara, 9; Kathy Willens, 20; The Herald/ Ivan Kashinsky, 23. *Peter Arnold Inc.:*
BIOS/ Klein & Hubert, 10, 32, 40, back cover; Phone Labat J.M. / F. Rouquette, 14; BIOS Gunther Michel, 35, 42;
Wegner, P., 39; PHONE Labat Jean-Michel, 43. *Minden Pictures:* Mark Raycroft, 18. *Kojiki Mutsu Images:* 41.

Editor: Karen Ang
Publisher: Michelle Bisson
Art Director: Anahid Hamparian
Series Designer: Elynn Cohen

Printed in Malaysia
6 5 4 3 2 1

Contents

1

Loyal Friends

Dogs and humans have worked and lived together for thousands of years. Images of dogs show up in ancient artworks and artifacts. These dogs guarded homes, helped humans hunt, worked in the fields, rescued travelers, or stayed inside as a well-loved part of a family.

Legendary Dogs

All across the world, big dogs have always had a special place in legends and mythology. The Ancient Greek poet Homer wrote a famous story about a hero named Odysseus. Odysseus had traveled far from home for many years, and when he returned the only one to recognize him was his faithful dog. This dog, Argos, became a symbol for loyalty.

Another example is the story of Hachiko, an Akita that lived in Japan in the 1920s with his owner, Professor Ueno. Every morning, Hachiko would

This mosaic—a piece of art made of tiles—is more than one thousand years old. Ancient Romans probably used dog mosaics to warn others that big dogs were guarding their homes.

An Akita's ears are supposed to stand straight up, but Hachiko's statue shows that one of his ears was floppy.

accompany Professor Ueno to the train station, where the professor would board the train to go to work. Hachiko would go back home during the day, but returned to the train station every evening to wait for Professor Ueno.

However, one day the professor passed away while he was at work. Though the professor did not come home that night, Hachiko waited for him at the station. The loyal Akita eventually went back home, but returned to the train station the next day to wait for his friend. This continued for several years. Many people who visited the station helped to care for the dog, giving him food and finding a place for him to sleep. No matter where Hachiko roamed during the day, when evening came, he went back to the station to wait for Professor Ueno. One of the professor's old students heard about Hachiko and wrote a story about him in a Japanese newspaper. Hachiko's story became famous. Today, a statue of Hachiko stands at Shibuya Train Station in Tokyo, Japan. Many people come to visit the statue, honoring the devoted big dog and the special bond between a dog and its owner.

Hard Workers

In cold regions around the world, many big dogs are used to pull sleds filled with people or supplies. Large dogs, such as Alaskan malamutes and Siberian huskies are most often used as sled dogs. The world's most famous sled dog race is the Iditarod in Alaska. This event honors the men, women, and dogs that courageously traveled through the freezing cold and snow to deliver much-needed supplies to towns and villages throughout Alaska.

Huskies and malamutes make good sled dogs because they have big muscles for pulling heavy objects. Their thick fur protects them from the cold and snow.

German shepherds are often used as police dogs.

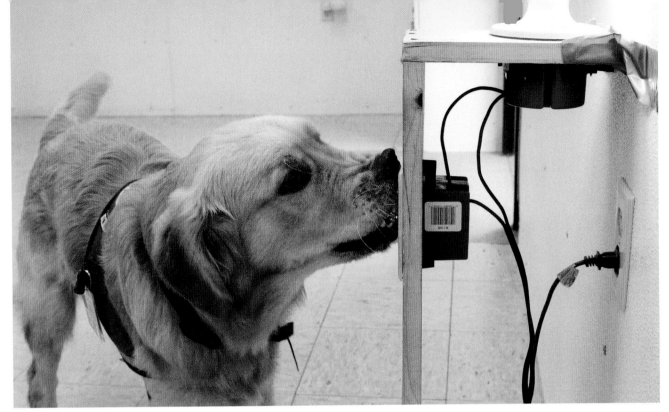

Service dogs are trained to help people with disabilities. This big dog is learning how to turn on light switches for its owner.

Throughout the world, many big dogs help people every day. Several different types of big dogs are used by police and security people to sniff out bombs or other dangerous things. Others are used as search-and-rescue dogs. Many big hounds and other dogs with good senses of smell and hearing are used to search for and help people who are missing or in danger.

Some big dogs are trained as seeing-eye dogs to help the blind, while others help people who are in wheelchairs or people with certain medical conditions. Therapy dogs are brought into hospitals or homes for the elderly to spend time with the people staying there. With their happy personalities and gentle manners, these big dogs help bring smiles to many faces.

2

Is a Big Dog Right
for You?

All big dogs start out as small and cute puppies. It is fun to hold and cuddle these little bundles of fur. In time, those little puppies will eventually grow into larger adult dogs. Having a big dog can bring great joy. But it is also a big responsibility and there are many important things to consider. Before bringing home a big dog, you should ask yourself and your family the following questions.

Do I Have Enough Time?

Having a pet requires a lot of time and patience. This is especially true for big dogs. Besides making time to feed and groom your dog, it is also important to spend time working and playing with your pet. All dogs need

Big dogs, such as this Leonberger, make excellent family pets.

Growing puppies, like this Vizsla, need a lot of room to run around and play. As big dogs get older, they will need even more space.

to have proper **socialization** with people and with other dogs. Dogs need to be trained to walk on a leash, listen to commands, and behave. Socialization and training is important so that dogs—and their humans—do not get hurt. You will need to set aside time every day to train your big dog.

Like people, all dogs need exercise to stay healthy. So you must also make time to play and exercise with your big dog. Exercising with the dog can include jogging together, taking brisk walks through the neighborhood, or tossing around a Frisbee or ball.

Do I Have Enough Space?

Big dogs need quite a bit of space. Not all big dogs need large, fenced-in backyards. But there should be a place nearby—a park or a field—where you and your dog can safely run and play.

A big dog bed provides your pet with a comfortable spot for sleeping or relaxing.

Many big dogs get along well with cats and other household pets. However, until you are sure they like each other, never leave your big dog alone with smaller pets.

Indoors, big dogs—with their large paws and even bigger bodies—can knock into furniture, doors, and walls if there is not enough space. They might also be underfoot, tripping their humans as they make their way through the home. Your big dog will also need a place to sleep, whether it is a dog bed on the floor or a comfortable **crate.**

If you have other pets, such as another dog or a cat or bird, you will need to be careful about introducing them to your big dog. Your dog might need his or her own space to get used to the new home. Many pet owners find that their multiple pets get along wonderfully, but it often takes some time for the animals to get used to each other. Before you get a big dog, you must make sure there is enough space in your home for everyone.

BIG DOG LAWS

In the United States, there are some laws and rules that have to do with owning big dogs. Some towns and cities do not allow residents to have certain types of big dogs. Additionally, some insurance companies—businesses that help protect you and your property—also have rules about owning big dogs. When considering a big dog, you should have your parents or guardians find out if there are any laws or rules that would apply to you and your new pet.

3

Choosing Your Big Dog

Once you and your family have made the decision to add a big dog to your family, there are many other choices to make. How old should the dog be? What kind of dog best suits your family? Where is the best place to get your big dog?

Puppy or Adult?

Puppies make wonderful pets. They are cute and cuddly, which is why many people are charmed by them. It is fun to get to know and bond with a puppy as it grows throughout the years. But a puppy might not be the right choice for everyone. Because puppies are young, they need their humans to

The first Saint Bernards worked as herding, hunting, and guard dogs for farmers in Switzerland. These lovable big dogs became famous for rescuing people lost on snowy mountains.

give them extra-special care. Since puppies are growing they need to be watched carefully so they do not get into trouble or get hurt. Many puppies do not like being left alone for long periods of time during the day. This can lead to messes in the house when the puppy has accidents or when the pup chews or tears up shoes, clothes, and furniture. (Some adult dogs can also behave this way.)

You will also need to spend a lot more time training your puppy. It needs to learn its name and basic commands. You must also housetrain your

Rottweilers are sometimes used to work on farms or to guard property. The puppy on the left is a few months old, while its friend on the right is about three years old.

puppy. A **housetrained** puppy is trained to go to the bathroom outside or in a specific spot indoors.

Older dogs also make excellent pets. Most older dogs have had some basic training, so you will not need to worry about teething, housetraining, or walking on a leash. In many cases, older dogs are not as active as puppies and can be left alone at home for longer periods of time. Families who are looking for quiet companions often prefer older dogs. But young or old, all big dogs require—and deserve—a lot of attention and love.

Big Dog Breeds

All domesticated dogs—dogs that are kept as pets—are related to wild dogs, such as wolves and coyotes. Thousands of years ago, humans and dogs started living together. People in ancient cultures used the dogs to help work in the fields or to protect homes. Eventually, dogs were also kept indoors and considered part of the family. Humans chose specific dogs for the animals' physical traits and personalities. They bred those dogs with other dogs to develop more specific characteristics. For example, a medium-sized dog that was good for hunting was bred with a different type of dog that was larger and stronger. The result was a new type of big hunting dog. This is one example of how different **breeds** or types of dogs developed. Some dog breeds can trace their roots back more than a thousand years. Other breeds have only developed in the last hundred years.

There are many big dog breeds. Each breed of dog has specific physical traits, such as long or short fur, long legs, big heads, or floppy ears. Though every single dog has its own unique personality, most dogs belonging to a certain breed share similar characteristics. For example, certain spaniels or retrievers are very active and need a lot of time to exercise, run, or swim. You should do careful research to learn about different breeds when you think about getting a big dog. A local **veterinarian**, or vet, is a good source for information. A vet can also suggest other places for you to research. There are many books and Web sites about specific breeds of dogs.

Attending local dog shows is another good way to learn about different breeds. Dog shows are special events that showcase specific breeds. The people who handle the dogs at the show are often happy to answer questions you might have about the breed. At a dog show you will get to see how different breeds look and how big they will grow.

While many families enjoy having a dog that is one specific breed—called a **purebred dog**—this is not

Dog shows give you a chance to learn about dog breeds that you would not commonly see, such as this Ibizan hound. This big breed has been around for thousands of years, and is commonly shown in ancient Egyptian artwork.

always the case. There are many big dogs that are **mixed breeds.** This means that their parents or grandparents belong to one or more different breeds. Many people who have mixed-breed dogs say they get the best traits of many breeds all in one package!

The American Kennel Club (AKC) system divides dog breeds—both big and small—into eight different groups. These are working dogs, hound dogs, sporting dogs, non-sporting dogs, herding dogs, terriers, toy dogs, and a miscellaneous group. The toy group has no big dogs. The terrier and miscella-neous groups have only a couple of big dog breeds.

Working Dogs

As their name suggests, dogs that belong to the working group were bred to perform specific jobs, such as guarding a home, pulling or carrying carts or material, or rescuing people. All of the breeds in the working group are big dogs. The Great Dane is one big dog breed that

Great Danes can be solid brown, white, black, gray, or a mixture of any of these colors.

was initially used as a loyal guard dog. A full grown Great Dane can be almost 3 feet tall—when measured from the bottom of the foot to the top of its shoulder—and can weigh more than 120 pounds! Many families who have Great Danes love living with these gentle giants. But like most working dogs, this big breed requires a lot of space, a lot of exercise, and a lot of training. Other familiar working dogs include the Doberman pinschers, Newfoundlands, Great Pyrenees, rottweilers, komondors, mastiffs, Saint Bernards, Siberian huskies, Alaskan malamutes, Akitas, giant schnauzers, and boxers.

Using his nose, this trained bloodhound has tracked down a cat from a neighboring farm.

Hound Dogs

Hound dogs were originally—and are still—used to help people hunt. Most hounds have a really good sense of smell, and are often called scent hounds. These hounds can track down other animals, missing children, or can even be trained to sniff out drugs, bombs, and other dangerous materials. One of the most popular scent hounds is the bloodhound. These big brown dogs have floppy ears and a lot of loose wrinkles on their faces. A bloodhound can grow to weigh more than 100 pounds. Other hounds include greyhounds, Afghans, foxhounds, coonhounds, wolfhounds, deerhounds, salukis, and Rhodesian ridgebacks.

Sporting Dogs

Big dogs that belong to this group are very physically active. Golden retrievers and Labrador retrievers are the most popular sporting dogs. There are several different types of retrievers and spaniels, and most of these big dogs love playing in the water. Some dogs, such as the Chesapeake Bay retriever, have a special **coat**—the fur on their bodies—that is ideal for being in the water. Vizslas, Weimaraners, and German pointers are just some of the other big sporting dog breeds.

GREYHOUNDS

Hounds are known for their speed. Many of these dogs have just the right body size and type to run far and fast. The fastest domesticated dog is the greyhound, which can run as fast as 45 miles per hour. Because of their speed, most greyhounds are bred and raised to be used in dog races. When the dogs are too old or too tired to race, many of the greyhounds are put up for adoption. Across the country, organizations devoted to finding homes for retired racers connect families with these lovable runners.

Most greyhound rescue organizations hold adoption events at large pet stores, malls, or public buildings. People are encouraged to meet the dogs, ask questions, and think about giving these retired racers happy homes.

Dalmatians are high-energy dogs. In order to be healthy and happy, they need to play and run around a lot.

Non-Sporting Dogs

Most non-sporting dogs are smaller breeds, though there are a few big dogs in this group. Dalmatians are easily recognizable by their white coats with black spots. These dogs have been in popular children's movies and are often seen as companions to firefighters across the country. Standard poodles, the larger version of the miniature poodle, are popular pets. Some are groomed to have interesting-looking coats, while other owners let the poodles' fur cover the dogs' entire bodies. During the 1980s and 1990s, John Suter, a dog-sled racer, used a pack of standard poodles in Iditarod races. Even though this type of dog was rarely used for pulling sleds, Suter loved

John Suter lines up his poodle team before a race in Chugiak, Alaska.

his poodles and knew they could work hard and do a good job. However, he had to stop racing the poodles because the rules of the race changed and poodles were no longer allowed to enter.

Herding Dogs

These dogs were bred to herd farm animals like sheep. These breeds have a lot of energy and are extremely intelligent. Collies, sheepdogs, and shepherds

25

Komondors are a type of Hungarian sheepdog. Their fur—which many say resembles a mop—is very thick and protects them from the cold.

are popular herding pets. Some families who have young children and herding dogs claim that the dogs often try to herd the kids and keep them in line!

Where Can I Find a Big Dog?

Once you have an idea of what kind of big dog you want, one of the next steps is to figure out where to get it. There are many places where you can adopt or buy a dog, but not all will be the right place for you. Careful consideration and research are the keys to finding the right dog from the right place.

Breeders

A dog breeder is a person who raises certain breeds of dogs. For example, there may be a breeder who raises only golden retrievers, while another raises only Great Danes. One way to find a good, reliable breeder is to ask a veterinarian. If you know someone who already owns the type of dog you want, you could find out which breeder they used. You can also find breeder information from local dog clubs or organizations. Many dog magazines have sections that list dog breeders by breed and by state. Breeders also place advertisements in newspapers and online.

A trustworthy breeder has been working with and raising that breed for several years. Responsible breeders breed dogs to celebrate and improve the breed. This means that they breed healthy dogs that will be shown in dog shows or become loving companions. A good breeder is not in the business just for money. Good breeders make sure that all their dogs are healthy. They bring their big dogs to the vet for all the necessary check-ups and shots. Most breeders sell puppies, though many will also have older dogs for sale.

Rescue Organizations and Shelters

Another source for finding a dog is through a dog rescue organization. People who are involved in these rescues take in dogs that are lost, abandoned, or no longer have owners who can care for them. Some rescue organizations only work with specific breeds, while others rescue dogs of all breeds and ages. In many cases, rescue organizations place the dogs in foster homes. These homes provide a safe and secure place for the dogs before they find new homes. Many rescue groups have ads in local papers, in veterinarians' offices, or have their own Web sites.

You can also adopt a dog from a local animal shelter. (Shelters are sometimes called humane societies or animal welfare societies.) Shelters are places that also keep animals that no longer have homes. Sometimes the dogs have been abandoned by their owners. In other cases, owners might not have been able to keep the dog because they developed allergies to the dog, had to move and could not bring the dog with them, or had a new baby in the household. Often, big dogs are brought to shelters because they grew larger than the owner expected or were too much for the owner to handle. Dogs in shelters are not necessarily bad dogs. Most are gentle and just need the right home.

Most of the dogs in shelters and humane societies are mixed breeds. All of them need loving homes.

Vet offices and pet stores sometimes have information about the different animal shelters. Many shelters are listed in the local phone books or have their own Web sites. Shelter Web sites often post pictures and descriptions of the animals that are looking for good homes. Once you find a shelter, you should visit it with your family. Take a look at what kinds of dogs they have. Most of the dogs in animal shelters will be mixed-breed dogs. Because so many people give up their big dogs when they realize how large they become, animal shelters usually have a large selection of big dogs. The people who volunteer at the shelter will help you figure out which big dog is right for you and your family.

Pet Stores

A lot of pet stores sell puppies. Some pet stores sell puppies from breeders who breed the puppies only for profit. These breeding facilities are often called puppy mills or puppy farms. Each puppy mill or farm can mass-produce hundreds of dogs each year. The dogs from puppy mills are kept in poor conditions and their parents are usually unhealthy. Even though they might not look like it, some puppies at the pet stores may be sick. Many people feel like they are "rescuing" the puppies from the pet store by buying them and bringing them home. In a way they are, since the puppies will go to good homes with people who will love and care for them. However, this encourages the puppy mills to continue to breed more puppies to fill up the empty cages in the stores.

Not all pet stores get their dogs from puppy mills. Some small stores get their puppies from local breeders who are responsible and careful about the puppies they breed and sell. Before buying a puppy from a store, be sure to do some research. Find out where the puppies come from.

Do Your Research and Ask Questions

Old or young, mixed breed or purebred, big dogs make excellent playmates.

No matter where you get your big dog from, it is important to do your research and ask a lot of questions. Find out as much as you can about the source, whether it is a breeder, shelter, or rescue organization. How long has this place been around? Do the people who work or volunteer there seem very knowledgeable?

When you visit a breeder, foster home, or the shelter, take note of the surroundings. Do the cages or kennels where the dogs are kept look clean? Are there too many dogs to fit into small spaces? Do the dogs look alert and active? Do many of the dogs look very ill?

When you are looking at a specific dog you might want to take home, you can ask some of the following questions:

- How old is the dog?
- Will the dog grow to be very big?
- Has the dog been checked by a veterinarian?
- Is the dog up to date on all of its shots?
- How much exercise does the dog get each day?
- How does the dog react to children?
- How does the dog get along with the other dogs?
- Does the dog get along with cats and other household animals?
- Is the dog housetrained?
- Has the dog had some training so that it walks on a leash or listens to commands?
- If the dog is in a shelter or foster home, why was the dog put there?
- How long has it been in the shelter or foster home?

Getting the answers to these questions, and then taking some time to think about them, will help you to bring home the **canine** companion that is perfect for you and your family.

4

Life with Your
Big Dog

The next step in welcoming a new big dog into your home is learning how to take care of it. Your dog will need food, water, toys, and a lot of love and patience.

Vet Visits

Before you bring home your big dog, you should schedule an appointment with a local vet. You should bring your dog to the vet as soon as you can. The vet will check your dog to make sure it is healthy and give it any shots or medication it may need. Plan on bringing your dog to the vet at least once or twice each year. A visit to the vet is a good opportunity to ask any questions you might have regarding your big dog's health and care.

A Siberian husky puppy cuddles with his new friend.

A mother and son bring their Weimaraner puppy to the vet for its shots. These shots will help protect the dog from many different illnesses.

Feeding

When you adopt or buy your big dog, you should ask what kind of diet the dog is on. Does the dog eat dry food (called kibble), canned dog food, or a mixture of both? How much and how often does the dog eat? You can continue to feed the dog that kind of food, or you can slowly switch the dog over to different food. A veterinarian can advise you on the type and amount of food your big dog should be eating. Dog food can be bought in pet stores and in almost all grocery stores.

Treats for your big dog may include dog biscuits or strips of dried meat prepared specifically for dogs. These treats can be given when you are playing with your dog or when the dog is being good. But too many treats can make a dog sick or overweight, so be careful.

Most veterinarians do not recommend giving your big dog table scraps, leftovers, or most types of human food. Dog food is made specifically to help the dogs grow properly and maintain the right weight. Feeding your dog human food can upset its stomach and make it overweight. Some human food is poisonous to dogs, so it is a good idea to avoid giving your dog any human food.

Like all living things, big dogs need water to survive. Your big

An Irish wolfhound takes a cool drink after spending the afternoon playing outside.

35

DANGER!

There are many foods, chemicals, plants, and household items that are dangerous or poisonous to dogs. If your big dog eats any of the following things, call your veterinarian or animal hospital immediately:

FOODS

- chocolate
- coffee or tea
- onions
- grapes and raisins
- human medication or vitamin supplements
- nuts
- mushrooms

PLANTS

- mistletoe berries
- lilies
- aloe
- azaleas
- daffodils
- foxglove

HOUSEHOLD ITEMS

- cleaning products like soap or bleach
- antifreeze (for cars)
- rubber bands
- string
- coins

- human toys—metal, plastic, small, or large
- glue
- moth balls
- pesticides used to kill bugs or rodents

dog should have access to a clean bowl of water throughout the day. This is especially important on hot days or after your dog has been exercising a lot. The water bowl must be refilled with fresh, clean water every day.

Grooming

How much grooming your big dog needs depends on what kind of dog you have. Dogs with really thick or shaggy coats will need to be brushed more often. This is especially true during the warm months when your dog may be

When the weather is warm, it is often easier to bathe your big dog outside. Bath time can be a fun activity for dogs and their owners.

shedding. Your big dog also needs baths to keep its fur and skin clean. You should always use shampoos or soaps that are made specifically for dogs. Human soaps and shampoos may make your dog sick or itchy. If your big dog needs to have its fur trimmed you can bring it to a groomer. These professionals have a lot of experience with dogs of all shapes and sizes.

Grooming your dog also includes keeping its nails short and cleaning its ears and teeth. Your veterinarian can help you with this.

Accessories

Besides food and water dishes, dog brushes, and shampoo, your big dog needs other supplies. All dogs should have a collar and a leash. The collar and leash gives you something to hold on to if you need to catch your dog or pull it away from dangerous situations. Many states have leash laws that require dogs to be on leashes whenever they are outside. Make sure that the collar and leash are big enough and strong enough for your big dog.

The collar is also used to hold an identification or ID tag for your dog. These tags can be specially made at pet stores or vet offices. The tags have information such as the dog's name, your last name, your home phone number, or your address. If your dog runs away or gets lost, this information will tell people how they can contact you. Some dog collars have the information printed on the collar instead of on a tag. Many pet owners also have a small ID chip placed beneath the dog's skin. The painless procedure is performed by a veterinarian. These chips contain a lot of useful

Make sure the collar and leash that you buy are strong enough for your big dog. Strong dogs, like this Bernese mountain dog, can break free from a thin or lightweight leash.

information about the dog and its owner. These chips cannot fall off the dogs like tags or collars.

Dogs like to have special places they can call their own. A dog bed or a dog crate can serve this purpose. Crates are good for young puppies or for dogs that are being introduced to a new environment. Keeping a dog in a crate while you are out of the house can prevent injuries to your dog. Crates also prevent messes for you to clean up around the house. As with all accessories for a big dog, you must be sure that the bed and crate are large enough to hold your big friend.

All dogs should learn basic commands, such as sit, stay, down, and come.

Socializing and Training

All dogs—especially big dogs—should be properly socialized. This means that the dog should learn to get along with other dogs and people outside of your family. You can do this yourself by carefully introducing a young puppy to other people and dogs. Older big dogs, however, require a little more work for socialization. Many dog training schools offer classes or programs that can help your dog get along with others. Proper socialization can help prevent a big dog from biting people or being **aggressive** toward people and other pets.

All dogs should have some training. Whether it is learning to sit or stay when told or coming when called, training is very important. For example, if your dog gets off its leash or runs away from you, calling its name and having it come back to you can save it from a dangerous situation. A big dog should also learn what it can and cannot do inside your house. Big dogs that are too wild and do not listen can crash into objects inside the house, hurting themselves or their owners. Dog training schools offer many levels of training for all kinds of dogs. A vet can also recommend training centers. Some large

You can also train your dog to do fun things like shaking your hand, rolling over, or fetching toys. This Akita is learning to bring a ball back to her owner.

pet stores offer weekly classes in the store. Training classes can be fun for both you and your dog. They are an excellent time for the two of you to get to know each other better.

Playing with Your Dog

Most dogs are naturally playful. Going for a run or romping around the yard with your big dog can be a lot of fun. You might have your dog chase after a big ball or Frisbee. Make sure the ball or Frisbee is strong enough to withstand the big teeth of your big dog. When playing or running outside, always be sure to stay in a secure area. A fenced-in yard or dog park are ideal places. Be careful not to throw the ball or Frisbee too close to a road or sidewalk. Most dogs do not know that they have to look out for cars, bicycles, or runners who might crash into them.

When you cannot play with your dog, it is a good idea to offer it toys that it can play with on its own. These might be plastic bones or squeaky toys. Do not give your big dog human toys. Pet stores sell a wide variety of toys made just

Many big dogs love to cuddle with their soft toys.

for big dogs. Just be sure that there are no small parts that the dog can swallow and choke upon.

You should try to spend a lot of time with your dog indoors. Many big dogs love to sit quietly while you pet them, scratch behind their ears, or rub their bellies. Some big dogs are happy to simply sit beside you while you work on your homework, read a book, or watch television.

With time, patience, hard work, and a lot of affection, a big dog is a truly great pet and can become one of your best friends.

Big dogs can bring a lot of love and happiness into your life.

Glossary

aggressive—An aggressive dog may be likely to bark at, attack, or bite people or other animals. Proper socialization and training can help prevent aggression and treat some aggressive dogs.

breeds—Specific types of dogs that share similar characteristics.

canine—Related to or having to do with dogs. *Canine* can also refer to a dog's long tooth.

coat—In dogs, it is the fur or hair on its body. For example, dogs can have long coats, short coats, or curly coats.

crate—A cage or kennel for a dog.

domesticated—Describes an animal that has been bred and tamed to become a pet (a dog or a cat), or to be kept by humans (farm animals).

housetrained—A dog that has been trained to go to the bathroom in a specific spot is housetrained.

mixed-breed dog—Dogs that belong to two or more different breeds.

purebred dog—A dog that belongs to one specific breed.

socialization—For dogs, it is the process of getting a dog used to interactions with people and other animals.

veterinarian—A doctor trained to treat different types of animals.

Find Out More

Books

Adelman, Beth. *Good Dog!: Dog Care for Kids.* Chanhassen, MN: Child's World, 2006.

Coren, Stanley. *Why Do Dogs Have Wet Noses?* Toronto: Kids Can Press, 2006.

Fogle, Bruce. *Dog Owner's Manual.* New York: DK Publishing, 2003.

George, Jean Craighead. *How to Talk to Your Dog.* New York: HarperCollins Publishers, 2000.

Jeffrey, Laura S. *Dogs: How to Choose and Care for a Dog.* Berkeley Heights, NJ: Enslow Publishers, 2004.

Rayner, Matthew. *Dog.* Milwaukee, WI: Gareth Stevens, 2004.

Web Sites

The American Kennel Club

http://www.akc.org/breeds
The American Kennel Club has a Web site that lists all the dog breeds that this organization recognizes. At this Web site, you can also find a list of breeders and breed rescue groups.

ASPCA's ANIMALAND

http://www.aspca.org/site/PageServer?pagename=kids_home
The American Society for the Prevention of Cruelty to Animals (ASPCA) sponsors this site for kids who want to learn more about pets. The Web site features games, activity sheets, cartoons, and a lot of information about caring for a pet.

Dr. P's Dog Training

http://www.uwsp.edu/psych/dog/dog.htm
This Web site has been set up by the University of Wisconsin to help you train your puppy or your dog. There are articles about how to housetrain your puppy, how to teach your dog commands, how dogs use their powerful sense of smell, and much more.

How to Love Your Dog

http://loveyourdog.com
Developed by a teacher and dog enthusiast, this Web site offers information about caring for a dog and the joys and hard work that come with responsible ownership.

About the Author

Joyce Hart is a freelance writer. Throughout her life, she has had many different types of dogs in her life—big and small. All of her dogs have been mixed breeds. Right now, Ms. Hart lives with Molly, a big mixed breed that is part German Shepherd and part who-knows-what. The first time Ms. Hart saw Molly at an animal shelter, she knew they would make great friends. Today, Molly is five years old and loves to go for long walks.

Index

Page numbers for illustrations are in **bold**.